FROM CHAOS TO CLARITY IN 7 STEPS

FROM CHAOS TO CLARITY IN 7 STEPS

Organize Your Life

JUDE HAWTHORNE

QuillQuest Publishers

CONTENTS

CHAPTER 1

Introduction

This is always step #1 because it's super important. Regardless of what changes you decide to implement, without some serious focus on your mindset, it'll be really hard to implement those changes long-term. In the last part of the series we discussed the big picture "Why." That post was designed to help you either maintain or re-discover your zest for life. If part of your dream is to break free from the bondages of the clutter in your life, then it's time to start getting super-focused. If it's clarity that you're after, then we need to first get super clear on what it is you're shooting for with your physical space - what does that end game look like? Are you after a peaceful retreat to relax at the end of the day, a functional workspace, a home primed for entertaining, or a space that inspires creativity?

What better time to tame the chaos in your life than the start of a new year? In a few weeks on the blog, I'll be diving headfirst into how to get your yucky, cluttered head clear and focused. So in preparation for that, I'm concluding my chaos series with the finale - which is about working on the space around you. Don't make the mistake of thinking that disorganization in your physical space doesn't affect you. It absolutely does - you're just less aware of the reasons why. When your physical world is a mess, your head has to work harder at focusing on what it really wants to do. Think of it like static on a phone line - when your world contains only what you love and use, your priorities come into sharp focus and suddenly you have a much clearer understanding of who you are and who you want to be. Plus, you'll feel a lot more freedom by simplifying. And we all crave that, don't we? So let's dig into some steps to get us closer to that simplified life.

CHAPTER 2

Assessing Your Current Situation

For example, here is a single list for the house: clean, maintain children's play and personal areas, prepare meals, do meal dishes, empty dishwasher, family laundry, meal shopping, reminder shopping (toiletries, fresh produce), storage, item replacement, maintenance, yard maintenance work, manage clothes and personal care, correspondence, schedule repairs and improvements, grow vegetables, stock up, clean the barn, garage order, tools maintenance, tidy up children's toys, children's school supplies purchasing, schedule regular and special maintenance for the vehicles, scheduled doggy wellness, organize TEOR. This isn't an exhaustive list and isn't for you to completely organize your entire house; this is more of writing your flylady list with a little more attention to the smallest details and in which you sort tasks by chronological frequency as much as possible ('once a day', 'several times a week', 'once a week', 'every 15 days', 'once a month', 'every 3 months', etc.). This will take you several days to list everything, to the smallest perceived task.

In the first step in overcoming chaos and choosing clarity, you're going to carefully look at your life – because you can't pick a destination until you know where you are, you can't maximize your potential until you clearly understand your tendencies and weaknesses. Think of this as the preliminary check-up so you can choose the best training plan for you at your current level of awareness. To truthfully assess all of your current responsibilities, duties, to-dos, and goals, it's best to use a multi-step process. For 30 days (or more!), create a list for each category in your life. Each day, you should assess one area: home, children, school, work, pleasure, addictions, if you own your own business, etc... Whatever roles you fulfill in your day-to-day life, add them to the assessment list.

CHAPTER 3

Setting Clear Goals

On top of writing it down, you need to be accountable. There are a couple of different strategies I recommend for holding yourself accountable. The first is to share your goals with friends and family. For a long time, Cary and I had our big goals (like having a pool and equipping it with a waterslide and palm trees) posted on the door. We had a goal of building out the outdoor kitchen, so we saved up for it and invested in a grill, some outdoor furniture, and a cooler for the outdoor patio. Whether you share with your friends and family or post your goals on sticky notes or a vision board, make them visible! Additionally, share your goals on social media. Trust me, if you post your goals in a Facebook group or on your Instagram, then someone will follow up and ask about your progress. Which means you should give props when other folks are making strides. Social media can be a great way to keep each other accountable. So hold your friends and family accountable, and have them hold you accountable in response.

If you feel like you can't get ahead, the problem is that you're not clear on exactly what you want. Write down what you're trying to achieve with your life. Are you looking to reach a certain income? If that's one of your goals, write that down. Are you trying to spend more quality time with your kids? Write that down. Trust me, writing it down is key. You're 42% more likely to achieve your goals if you write them down. As you set your goals, make sure they're SMART: specific, measurable, achievable, relevant, and time-bound. It's great to have big goals, but we must set small goals along the way to keep ourselves motivated. It's easy to lose sight of our vision if we get bogged down by the messy day-to-day tasks of entrepreneurship. Establish daily, weekly, and monthly goals.

CHAPTER 4

Creating an Action Plan

Like many of you, I also have "eureka" moments when I am driving, humming in the shower, or just meditating on a problem in the back of my mind. I completely underrate a lot of the ideas that manifest themselves to me, and have thus incorporated various nooks in my productivity system so that I can quickly capture these ideas and the triggering context in which they occurred. When my mind is racing, it takes only a few seconds to quickly capture an idea onto an action list rather than drafting something more formal. As a good friend of mine once told me, "just because you think it's a great idea, doesn't mean you should drop everything else." It's important to put these ideas in their place so that they are never lost, but doesn't necessarily mean having to embellish every detail behind the idea.

In the realm of personal productivity, I often find that I have spent months, even years, working very hard to test, try and tweak various systems to see what works best for me. And after all this time, the one solution that has worked consistently to categorize and prioritize all the action items that I tally is an action tag that I have named "Process Step." Throughout every engagement or meeting I have, I take down copious notes just to confirm that my customers' objectives are at the heart of whatever it is that I am working on, and then I move those objectives through specific actions. These actions have a resolution, be it a business document, a phase exit review, a punch list for corrective actions or an in-depth Siemens application demonstration. I have found that what is absolutely crucial is to get the "To Do" item or task out of the actionable or goal-driven mode and into this process-driven mode as quickly as possible. The underlying message is not that the task has been "accelerated," but that the context in which the task is actionable is clearly understood and documented so I can document the prompt and formalized objective of the "To Do" that I use. These explicit goals allow me to better organize the idea into what is needed and quickly derive the document standardization to complete the simplest way possible without compromising quality.

CHAPTER 5

Implementing Effective Systems

Scannable and Expensify are my go-tos for paper receipts and all of my receipts come to my email in real-time. I can also use Expensify to scan and keep paper receipts for up to 5 days. Loyal readers know that I save all of my online receipts under the e-folder for the name of the company. For any category specific or very sensitive receipts, I will make a sub-folder and include the date and price of the item, no matter how small. If it's an e-receipt, I save everything either in Dropbox or Evernote. For larger folders, I make sure that there's a year prefix and then either save everything in January or December. Even now, everything I spend is saved in those two folders and everything is easy to answer tax-related questions.

Finally, getting organized means one thing: implementing effective systems. Here's the deal: when you find a new piece of information, an e-receipt, a business card, do you scan it and save it in your Gmail folder for 2014 followed by "Bills" and then the subfolder "January", "February", "March", "April", etc.? And why are you saving all your receipts in an e-directory as a once-a-month process?

What if you or your business is audited 11 months later? Ugh. It's enough to make you feel disorganized every single day! Instead, automate, automate, automate.

CHAPTER 6

Maintaining Consistency
and Discipline

Make sure you have a friend (no matter old or new) that has the same goal as yours. You know, whenever you feel doubtful and lazy about the things that you have planned, it is the best time to talk to him/her. Before they persuade you to the wrong way that they feel is best! Perhaps. Although I do it alone and I love sharing, but I suggest you do what I wrote in the sentence above. Most of your best friends are likely to love you with all their hearts. It feels like sometimes, for them, it is better for you to relax and show your potential someday, hopefully. Any burden, problems, and a good deal of fun should be shared. Keep on telling, about. A., B., C., or you would not write a novel in a single time.

First, you need to make sure that from now on, you are going to maintain consistency and discipline. All your hard work and the time you have dedicated to organize everything need to be monitored. Let me tell you, it is not easy! Sometimes, you will feel lazy to excite yourself with all the plans that you have decided. You might feel you are ready to quit. Don't! That is the main reason you need to have a little bit of discomfort around. There are times that you have to be tough with yourself. We, people, tend not to realize that changes need to be hard but good. That is what Pevita Pearce said. You might feel like this when you have to reject the plan to go out at night when all your friends want to invite you. You know there are still stuff waiting for you. No, you have to say. No matter what, always believe in what you believe, and not trying to persuade by others. Most of them come from their jealousy.

CHAPTER 7

Sustaining Long-Term Organization

Schedule short periods into your life on a regular basis to help maintain organization. It may be one day cleaning in common areas, a few minutes doing laundry, a short review of your files, a review of your clothes once a week, even a few minutes to store what is out of place in the kitchen every day. Your "Time Together" helps you to maintain order is a good way of organizing your "life together". This leads to a rewarding partnership with your children. It can also be something like mentally reviewing your current style to consider donating the clothes that you no longer need. Always aim to keep your space full of energy. In other times, you can schedule larger projects and attend home organization meetings so you get more visibility, attention, and commitment. Redo things in your life. Organization is not a goal but a lifestyle. Regularly perform regular in-depth maintenance, plus reorganization, remodel, and cleanup to make your system more attractive, efficient, and enjoyable to use.

This lifestyle change won't happen overnight. Knowledge, re-inforcement, and reminders can help. Do three things: keep organizing, develop good organizational habits, maintain order, and deal with information as it comes. Be efficient; invest a few minutes at a time for urgent tasks or even a few seconds to take the first step. If you follow the "a place for everything and everything in its place" rule and find concrete objects that require your attention in your life, or do it immediately file, you won't have to organize other areas of your life unless something has moved out of order - things are kept away from their places.

Milton Keynes UK
Ingram Content Group UK Ltd.
UKHW040329031224
452051UK00011B/317

9 798330 581207